Infectious

Volume 1

Tonia D Benas

Make Your Dash Count LLC
Published in Acworth, Georgia

Unless otherwise indicated, Scripture quotations are from the King James Version® Copyright © 1982 Thomas Nelson, Inc. Used by permission. All rights reserved.

Scripture quotations labeled AMP are from the Amplified Bible, copyright © 2015 by the Lockman Foundation. Used by permission. (www.Lockman.org)

Dedication

This book is dedicated to the powerful praying women in my life who are a part of my tribe and help sharpen me. I am forever grateful for their prayers, love and support. It is also for women who need to be empowered to be the best version of themselves on a daily basis. It is possible.

Introduction

My purpose in writing this is to empower others to positively impact other people. No matter how small the gesture, it can produce huge dividends or returns, both for you and the person that you have impacted. If you feel led to help someone, give a hug, an encouraging word, or to just be there for them, know that it is not in vain. And if that person never returns the favor or "rewards" you, so to speak, that is okay. God will reward you. Just keep being obedient and sharing His love with others. It will not return to you void. Keep planting those seeds of positivity and watch your harvest grow to overflow.

So many things <u>infect us</u> on a daily basis - both good and bad - whether it is the news, television shows, commercials, the radio, social media, or other people. We are **infected** and **affected** in some way, shape or form. It is imperative that we are mindful of what we allow in our spirit, and how we respond to it or let it shape us. The more good you put in, the more good you get out.

What things in your life do you need to limit that are affecting you negatively? What opinions or labels have others put on you that you believed and allowed to become your truth? Where did you stop growing because you became what other people said about you?

In this devotion, you will find life lessons and nuggets that I have learned along the journey. I share them with you in the hopes that each day, you can have a little positivity poured into your spirit, and be encouraged to make the most of each day.

Infectious is a movement. It is a challenge to be the best you that you can be. To strive to impact others, to leave a positive impression and residue on them, that remains whether you are present or not. It ignites a chain reaction that compels them to do the same or better, creating their own infectious legacy, and continuing yours!

Brand New Year, Brand New You

It's a new year, a new day. Most people have resolutions, new mindsets, things they are going to do. While others feel that their past has left them no chance of a future and, therefore, no hope, no joy. That is simply not true. Each day is a chance to start anew, to try again. Don't try to tackle a whole year's journey in one day. Take it one day at a time, and each day, choose happiness, joy, love; choose God. Then, as your days turn to weeks and years, you will have less regrets and more great memories.

~~~~~~

Day One

Today is a brand new day! How are you going to approach it? You get to decide if it will be a productive day or not. You get to decide if you will give your best, do your best and serve in excellence - or not. No one else can decide for you. This is the kick off to your week. Begin with the end in mind and then, work diligently to progress towards that, and enjoy the milestones and wins along the way. When Friday arrives, what will you want to have accomplished by then? Get going today to attain that goal!

Better is the end of a thing than the beginning thereof: and the patient in spirit is better than the proud in spirit.
Ecclesiastes 7:8

Reflection: What do you want to accomplish by Friday of this week?

Day 2

168 hours. That is the amount of time each of us is given every single week. We choose how we spend it. How we spend it, determines the direction that we will go. Where is your life headed? If you are unsure or not where you want to be or haven't yet accomplished what you desire - sit down and write out what you are doing with your time. I am certain that you will find plenty of time to be more productive and intentional about who and what you give your time to. Start with today. How will you spend the next 24 hours? What will you do better or differently? Less of? More of? No time like the present. Let's go! Happy Tuesday!

To everything there is a season, and a time to every purpose under the heaven.
Ecclesiastes 3:1

Reflection: How will you spend the next 24 hours?

Day 3

Love God. Love yourself. Love others. Always in that order. Determine what difference you will make today. Decide what you are grateful for. Use it to make the most of today.

It is a gift that you woke up this morning, so don't let the day go to waste. Feelings are temporary. It is okay to feel them and process through them, but don't allow it to captivate you and hold you hostage for an extended period of time.

This is the day which the Lord hath made; we will rejoice and be glad in it.
Psalm 118:24 KJV

Reflection: What is one thing that you can do to make the most of your day today?

Day 4

Have a faith filled day. Guard your heart and set the atmosphere around you. Don't let the mood swings and continual emotional changes of others affect you. You get to decide how you feel and how you will respond to everything that happens around you.

Above all else, guard your heart, for everything you do flows from it.
Proverbs 4:23

Reflection: How can you guard your heart today?

Day 5

Remember that you are not alone. You are human. God is fully capable of carrying you, caring for you and being your strength. Allow Him to be, so that you don't burn out or pass out. Give it to God and let Him guide you. You don't have to figure it all out yourself or come up with all of the answers. Rest in Him. Keep moving. Keep working. Trust Him for the results and the progress. Faith and works go together.

Thus also, faith by itself, if it does not have works, is dead.
James 2:17

Reflection: What are you believing God for? Have you taken any steps of faith towards that?

Day 6

There are people that we meet in life that may not always meet our requirements. They may not look according to our expectations, or act according to our expectations, but one thing we must remember is that God made us all unique and different on purpose. None of us are the same so we're not going to all look the same or act the same or do things the same way.

We must continually appreciate those differences in one another. Your strength may be my weakness. My strength may be your weakness. So we complement each other. God loves us all, no matter what size or shape we come in, and we should do the same thing. Practice unconditional love today. I challenge you to accept other people. Maybe it's not the person that everyone in the office talks to. Maybe it's the person that is usually quiet and keeps to themselves. Reach out to them today. Put yourself in their shoes. How would you want someone to respond to you?

A generous person will prosper; whoever refreshes others will be refreshed.
Proverbs 11:25

Reflection: How will you impact lives today?

Day 7

"Share your story, because you know how it feels, so you want to pour back into others because you would want someone to pour back into you."
Randi Chanel Person₁

What is your story? Do you know it? What would it take for you to share it, or who could you share it with that it may help or bless them? You could start a journaling habit, or write it an email to yourself, or a text message to yourself.

Just start writing it, so that you can share it when the time is right. Start with bullet points or an outline, and then, write as it comes to you. It doesn't have to be all at once. Set a timer for 15 minutes. Put down your phone, turn off the television, get rid of all other distractions, and just brain dump. Write until the timer goes off. You can continue to build on this, but **you have to at least start**, in order to have something to build on.

And the Lord answered me, and said, write the vision and make it plain upon tables, that he may run that readeth it.
Habakkuk 2:2

Reflection: Write at least two sentences about your story or one goal today.

Day 8

As you begin your day today, maintain your peace and your confidence in yourself. You matter. You are loved. You are enough. You are beautiful in every single way! That's how God sees you & you should see yourself that way, too! Never forget Whose you are.

The Lord shall fight for you, and ye shall hold your peace.
Exodus 14:14

Reflection: Repeat this scripture over and over until you believe it. Is your peace worth protecting?

Day 9

Life is totally what you make of it. It's up to you to decide how it turns out! You can waste time complaining about it or get up and make some changes. It is all in your mindset and perspective. That is where the enemy attacks you and tries to throw you off course and cause you to lose focus.

Equipped for battle is the only mindset you need. Then, you will always be prepared!

Finally, my brethren, be strong in the Lord, and in the power of His might. Put on the whole armor of God, that ye may able to stand against the wiles of the devil.
Ephesian 6:10-11 KJV

Reflection: What changes will you make today to be a better version of you?

Day 10

Life changes quickly from one day to the next, but Jesus is the same yesterday, today, and forever. Let Him be your rock, anchor, strength, shield, source, and everything else that you need. God's got you. Find your joy in Him each and every day, during the good and the bad; the happy and the sad. He always wants to spend time with you, and He is always there. His line is never busy.

I love them that love me, and those that seek me early shall find me.
Proverbs 8:17

Reflection: How will you anchor yourself in God today?

Day 11

Use today to bring God glory and to share your gifts and talents with those around you. Your purpose is greater than you think. With God, all things are possible. It's never too late to try again, to start over. The only opinion that matters is His. He is the only One you will stand before, so why worry about what anyone else thinks?

Stir up your gift! No fear here. God has equipped you. Proceed in faith. He will guide you every step of the way.

Don't let the midnight hours intimidate you. God's light is always shining.

Wherefore, I put thee in remembrance that thou stir up the gift of God, which is in thee by the putting on of my hands. For God hath not given us a spirit of fear; but of power, and of love, and of a sound mind.
2 Timothy 1:6-7

Reflection: Which of your gifts can you stir up today?

Day 12

I pray that you have uncommon favor today and that doors open for you to propel you into your greater. God has already ordered your steps. All you have to do is follow the path and trust His guidance - especially when you don't understand and don't have all the answers. You may not know how or when, but you always know WHO!

A man's heart deviseth his way: but the Lord directeth his steps.
Proverbs 16:9

Reflection: What steps will you take today?

Day 13

The only opinion that matters is God's opinion of you, and your opinion of you. In life, you will encounter countless opinions of other people. Your self-worth, value, purpose and destiny are not determined by their opinion. God already placed value in you before He formed you in your mother's womb. He thinks very highly of you. Now, it's just a matter of how you view yourself. Don't let the opinions of others taint your view of self. You are the only you that you have. Allow God to finish His work in you. Don't abort the mission or give up too soon.

I pray that today is a fabulous day, that you are productive, determined and focused. May it be your best day yet!

For it is God which worketh in you, both to will and to do of His good pleasure.
Philippians 2:13

I will praise You, for I am fearfully and wonderfully made, marvelous are Your works, and that my soul knows very well.
Psalm 139:14

Reflection: What is your opinion of yourself? Think through this and see where you need to make adjustments in your viewpoint of self.

Day 14

When we receive a word or promise from God, it is important to hold onto it and remember that His word does not return void. God knows the end from the beginning and that word or promise, is usually the manifestation at the end of a journey or process. Hold on to your promise during the waiting period; check your attitude, posture and praise. Maintain your hope and trust God. He will bring it to pass.

Do not trust in temporary, earthly things, but solely in the Eternal God and Savior! His name is Jesus!

So shall My word be that goes forth from My mouth; it shall not return to Me void, but it shall accomplish what I please, and it shall prosper in the thing for which I sent it.
Isaiah 55:11

Reflection: What promise from God are you holding onto?

Day 15

How well do you listen? Do you listen intentionally? Do you hurry the person along? Do you give them your full attention? Do you listen for God's voice and silence all others?

Listening, real listening, takes discipline. The ability to let go of your agenda and establish pure motives, so that you can understand what is being said to you and respond, instead of react. Today, practice listening and responding. Choose not to react. A soft answer turns away wrath.

So then, my beloved brethren, let every man be swift to hear (quick to listen), slow to speak, slow to wrath; for the wrath of man does not produce the righteousness of God.
James 1:19-20

Reflection: How can you practice listening and responding today?

Day 16

Light shines brightest when it is surrounded by darkness. It doesn't dim itself or hide or become darkness itself. The same goes for you. You may be the only light that others see. It is okay to be yourself. You don't have to be a replica of anyone else. Just Be You and help others' lights to shine brighter because of your influence and acceptance of them just as they are. Help them to climb higher. Iron sharpens iron.

As iron sharpens iron, so one person sharpens another.
Proverbs 27:17 NIV

Reflection: How can you sharpen someone else today?

Day 17

Things don't always go according to the way that you planned it. Sometimes, life throws us curve balls and the unexpected. It is in those times that we must trust and rest in God; the unknown can be scary, but God has us covered and it's never a surprise to Him. Nothing is too hard for Him; even when it is unbearable to us.

As you walk through today and the various things happening all around, focus on God, the good He has done and who He is. Let that carry you through your day. Be grateful. God's got you.

I will say of the Lord, He is my refuge and my fortress: My God,
in Him will I trust.
Psalm 91:2

Reflection: How can you keep your focus on God today?

Day 18

What is your top desire? Who do you seek first? What is your
main priority?

Knowing the answers to these questions, can help you to discover
and pinpoint who you are and what you will do and accomplish.
Asking God first and seeking his will for your life, helps give you
further clarity and direction. He created you, so no one can tell
you better than He can. Start your day with him every day, even if
just for five minutes. Time spent with God is always time well
spent.

But seek ye first the kingdom of God, and all His righteousness,
and everything else will be added unto you.
Matthew 6:33

Reflection: Who or what will you seek first today? Everyday?

Day 19

To God be the glory! In life, our paths have already been prewritten. Our choices and decisions we make determine our journey along the way. Sometimes, it seems like we are going in circles, and getting nowhere.

The important thing is to take steps forward, one at a time if necessary. Don't quit. Don't stop moving. Keep the momentum. God will be with you every step of the way!

The steps of a good man are ordered by the Lord: and He delighteth in his way. Though he fall, he shall not be utterly cast down: for the Lord upholdeth him with His hand.
Psalm 37:23-24

Reflection: What steps can you take today to move forward in God's plans for you?

Day 20

Time is one of our most valuable assets. How we spend it matters. Plan time for work, time for play, time for self care. It is all necessary and vital in order for you to show up every day as your best self.

So, how are you showing up? How are you spending your time? If you are feeling drained, tired, overwhelmed, or are procrastinating on several areas in your life, you need to sit down, plan out and assess your time. Maybe you started off good, and then you got off track. That is okay. Get back on track today, and keep going. Happy Planning!

My times are in Thy hand: deliver me from the hand of mine enemies, and from them that persecute me.
Psalm 31:15

Reflection: How will you spend the time that God has given you?

Day 21

Loving others can be hard, especially when we feel that they don't deserve it. But God always loves us - even when we don't deserve it. Extend grace today, have compassion and share joy. You may be the only positive that someone else sees and experiences.
Love God, Love Yourself, and Love Others. Always in that Order.

Jesus said unto him, "Thou shalt love the Lord thy God with all thy heart, and will all thy soul, and with all thy mind. This is the first and greatest commandment. And the second is like unto it, thou shalt love thy neighbor as thyself.
Matthew 22:37-39

Reflection: Only when you love God can you love yourself, and then in turn love others. How are you showing love today?

Day 22

Your job does not define you. Your value comes from within. You bring the value with you each and everyday when you show up as the best version of you.

Are you bringing your whole self to the work that you are doing? If not, why not? You have something in you that other people need. Let everything you do be done in love as unto the Lord. Use the gifts He has given you to make a difference in your workplace, home, neighborhood, and in those around you.

And whatsoever ye do, do it heartily, as to the Lord, and not unto men; knowing that of the Lord ye shall receive the reward of the inheritance: for ye serve the Lord Christ.
Colossians 3:23-24

Reflection: How can you serve everyone today as unto the Lord?

Day 23

There are times that we try to hold onto things that it is time for us to let go of. We try to prop open a door that God is trying to close or we try to do things in our own strength. Those times are when we find ourselves toiling.

When it is draining you and pulling all of your energy, it is usually not His will. God wants you to have sweatless victories because you are already victorious! Rest in and trust His plan for your life. He's got you covered. If He is telling you to let go, He knows far better than you do. It may hurt or be difficult temporarily, but what He has for you will be much greater than whatever you had to give up.

A time to get, and a time lose; a time to keep, and a time to cast away.
Ecclesiastes 3:6

Reflection: What is God telling you to let go of today?

Day 24

Facing your fears can be scary, even difficult at times. I have found that it is often a trick of the enemy to distract you, throw you off course, break your focus.

In those moments, breathe. Deep breaths. Focus on something positive. Play worship music. Read. Renew your mind. You can overcome. You can do this. God's got you.

For God hath not given us a spirit of fear; but of power, and of love, and of a sound mind.
2 Timothy 1:7

The Lord is my light and my salvation; whom shall I fear? The Lord is the strength of my life; of whom shall I be afraid?
Psalm 27:1

Reflection: God is with you, you do not have to be afraid. Repeat these scriptures every time a fear rises up in you.

Day 25

There are some things that experience will teach you, that an education can't. Sometimes your life experiences can teach you profound wisdom and give you insight that can't be taught. Not to take away from the value of education; just simply saying to use what you've learned to make you better and wiser.

Get wisdom, get understanding; forget it not; neither decline from the words of my mouth. Forsake her not, and she shall preserve thee: love her, and she shall keep thee. Wisdom is the principal thing; therefore, get wisdom: and with all thy getting, get understanding.
Proverbs 4:5-7

Reflection: What have life experiences taught you that you can use to do and be better right now? How can you help other people do the same?

Day 26

You have the power and ability to set the atmosphere around you. It doesn't matter if you messed up or fell yesterday; today is a new day! Determine what you will do and accomplish; how, why and when!
What impact will you have when you arrive? Will anyone notice your presence? Will your presence cause a shift or increase in the room that is positive or negative?

But ye are a chosen generation, a royal priesthood, an holy nation, a peculiar people; that ye should shew forth the praises of Him who hath called you out of darkness into His marvelous light.
1 Peter 2:9

Reflection: Will your presence cause a shift or increase in the room that is positive or negative?

Day 27

Whenever things and situations come against you, you have a choice to either break under the pressure, or stretch to your fullest capacity. It's a choice. Choose wisely.

No weapon that is formed against you shall prosper; and every tongue that shall rise against thee in judgment thou shalt condemn. This is the heritage of the servants of the Lord, and their righteousness is of me, saith the Lord.
Isaiah 54:17

Reflection: Will you stretch to your fullest capacity and grow today? In this season?

Day 28

Many things vie for our attention on a daily basis. We are
constantly pulled in several different directions. What do we
prioritize or give our time and attention to?
So many decisions to make and choices given. It can be
overwhelming. Breathe. Rest in God. Let Him lead and guide you
through your day. Ask Him where your focus should be.
Complete the things that you can. Maintain your peace. Don't fret
over the things that you can't control. Your sanity and peace
matter.

*Thus saith the Lord, thy Redeemer, the Holy One of Israel; I am
the Lord thy God which teacheth thee to profit, which leadeth
thee by the way that thou shouldest go.*
Isaiah 48:17

Reflection: Which way is God leading you today?

Day 29

Have you ever been so hungry for God? Had such a great desire to accomplish what He sent you to do?

I can't stop thinking about it. Purpose is banging on the door. Every step taken is one step closer. You don't have to have it all together. You don't have to have all of the answers. You don't have to have all of the resources. You just have to have faith in God, and trust Him to guide you every step of the way. He will be right there with you! Start. Right. Now. It's not too late! Let's go!!! Someone needs what you have!

Trust in the Lord with all thine heart; and lean not unto thine own understanding. In all thy ways acknowledge Him, and He shall direct thy paths.
Proverbs 3:5-6

Reflection: What great desire has God placed in your heart to accomplish?

Day 30

It's a brand new day! Do you know what that means? It's a fresh opportunity to be a better you. To make better decisions. Better choices. Yesterday is gone.

What are you in expectancy for today?! What do you want or need God to show up and do?! Wait for it. Praise Him in advance like it's already done. Go after everything He has for you!

For if the readiness is there, it is acceptable to what a person has, not according to what he does not have.
2 Corinthians 8:12

Reflection: Praise God in advance like it's already done!

Day 31

God has not given us a spirit of fear, but of power, love and a sound mind. We may not have all of the answers, or any, for that matter; but we do know the One who does have all of the answers. We must lean into and trust Him, sometimes blindly. When everything around you doesn't make sense, and you can't justify or explain it, go to God. With every care, every thought, every feeling. He can give you comfort, peace and direction. Lean on Him. He will carry you.

And whatever you ask in prayer, you will receive, if you have faith.
Matthew 21:22

Reflection: Only believe. God's got you.

Day 32

Great morning to you! This is the day the Lord has made. We will rejoice and be glad in it. Even when it is cloudy, the sun is always shining above the clouds. You can be the sunshine that brightens someone's day. Set the atmosphere around you and leave it more positive than you found it.

This is the day that the Lord has made; we will rejoice and be glad in it.
Psalm 118:24

Reflection: How can you brighten someone else's day today?

Day 33

Today, I am at a loss for words. I'm stuck between staying focused, giving up and falling apart. Transition is not always easy. Nor is being stretched. I choose to hang on to Jesus, and not let go. I need more of Him.

I encourage you today, to hold on in the waiting. Even when God doesn't move in your timing and according to your plans, He still has it covered. Trust Him through the process.

In all circumstances, take up the shield of faith, with which you can extinguish all the flaming darts of the evil one.
Ephesians 6:16

Reflection: Hold on in the waiting. Speak God's word and His truth out loud to increase your faith and strengthen your joy.

Day 34

Many times, things are out of our control. How we choose to respond and fully trust God is the only thing that we can control. So when life happens, take a deep breath; pause and refocus. The interruptions, distractions, slow drivers, missed appointments - they all serve a purpose. Realign your focus and look up - raise the level of your perspective and see the bigger picture. God's got you. None of it is a surprise to Him. Rest in Him.

I have been crucified with Christ. It is no longer I who live, but Christ who lives in me. And the life I now live in the flesh, I live by faith in the Son of God, who loved me and gave Himself for me.
Galatians 2:20

Reflection: Ask God to help you see things through His viewpoint and perspective. Kingdom minded focus.

Day 35

Good morning to you. Good? Why, because this is the day that the Lord has made; we shall rejoice and be glad in it. You woke up this morning, so you are blessed to still be here. Now, you have an opportunity to praise God and give Him the honor that He is due. To be a blessing to other people and to walk in purpose.

What has God told you to do that you haven't done yet?

What has He told you to say, that you haven't said yet?

What instruction has He given you, that you haven't completed yet?

By faith, Noah, being warned by God concerning events as yet unseen, in reverent fear, constructed an ark for the saving of his household. By this, he condemned the world and became an heir of the righteousness that comes by faith.
Hebrews 11:7

Reflection: Today, focus on answering those questions. Set your mindset for the day and what you want to get out of it. What will you want to have accomplished by the end of the day today? Begin with the end in mind, and choose your main three items for today. Just three. Work to knock out those three things, and don't forget to make time for Jesus, for yourself and for others. It's your time; spend it wisely. Schedule accordingly.

Day 36

God gives you a word. You are excited about it and embrace it, commit it to memory. For a while, you are running after it, and hopeful, believing in expectancy for great things. As time passes, your hope dwindles a little, but you just know it is coming to pass soon.

Later on, you start to doubt. Is God really going to do that? Maybe He changes His mind. Maybe I didn't do enough of this, or do enough of that. Maybe I missed my opportunity and it is no longer my time.

Wrong answer! God is not man that He should lie and His word will never return to Him void.

God is not man, that he should lie; neither the son of man, that he should repent: hath he said, and he shall he not do it? or hath he spoken, and shall he not make it good?

Numbers 23:19

So shall my word be that goeth forth out of my mouth: it shall not return unto me void, but it shall accomplish that which I please, and it shall prosper in the thing whereto I sent it.

Isaiah 55:11

Jesus said unto him, if thou canst believe, all things are possible to him that believeth. And straightway the father of the child cried out, and said with tears, Lord, I believe; help thou mine unbelief.

Mark 9:23-24

Reflection: When you start to doubt God and the word that He has given to you, <u>I want you to meditate on these three scriptures</u>. **Repeat the first two to silence the lies of the enemy. Repeat the last one to increase your faith and ask God to help you to remember to trust in Him and what He can do** in the supernatural, not the reality that you see in front of you.

Day 37

Joshua 1:9 reminds us that God is with us wherever we go and that we don't have to be afraid or discouraged. Life is happening all around us and it can be easy to get scared, be swayed, or walk in fear. Keep your focus on Jesus and know that He is with us always. Be encouraged today.

Have not I commanded thee? Be strong and of a good courage; be not afraid, neither be thou dismayed: for the Lord thy God is with thee whithersoever thou goest.
Joshua 1:9

Reflection: How can you keep your focus on Jesus today?

Day 38

Sometimes, we ask God for answers that He has already given us - we just didn't accept what He said and figured (or hoped) that He would change His mind. Sometimes, you know the answer - you just have to be okay with it and trust that God knows best.

Trust in the Lord with all your heart, and lean not on your own understanding; in all your ways acknowledge Him, and He shall direct your paths.
Proverbs 3:5-6

Reflection: Wherever you are stuck or stagnant, assess and reflect on whether or not God has already given you an instruction to follow. Then, follow that instruction.

Day 39

In the natural realm, seasons change. We have Spring, Summer, Fall, and Winter. It directs time, the calendar, holidays, and even the weather.

The same thing happens in the spiritual realm as well. You have to be in tune with God and in relationship with Him to recognize when the season is changing. Sometimes, it is winter time, but we were too busy playing and living it up in the Summer, that we wasted the Fall and did not prepare for the hibernation or isolation of winter or the lack season.

Other times, we got comfortable and complacent, and when it was time to change, we weren't ready. God was, but we dragged our feet, thinking that we knew better or could wait a while longer. Well, I'm telling you that the SEASON IS CHANGING NOW! You can't get to where you are going or to desire to go, by doing the same thing that you have always done.

When one door closes, another opens. God OWNS them all! If He opened the current door, why do you think He can't open another one? Oh ye of little faith. God desires to do GREAT things THROUGH YOU. But He needs you in place in order to do them.

If you are tired of hoping, wishing; tired of struggling and tarrying, and you want to fulfill the purpose that God has given you, the time is now. You have to be ALL in. Even if He does it completely differently than you expected or thought that He would do it. You have to trust the process.

What season are you coming out of? What season are you going into? The seasons of God don't work the same way as they do in the natural. It could be hot today, and cold tomorrow. Recognize the season that you are in. Respond accordingly.

For everything there is a season, and a time for every matter
under heaven.
Ecclesiastes 3:1

Reflection: What season are you in?

Day 40

You don't know what people have been through. Everyone has a story, a struggle, a calling and a purpose. So get down off of your high horse and stop judging someone based solely on the surface level that you see, or the highlight reels that they post.

You weren't with them in their prayer closet. You don't know the conversations that they've had with God. You don't know what He is working on in them. They are His child, too.

This is why scripture tells us in Matthew 7:5 ESV "You hypocrite. First, take the log out of your own eye, and then, you will see clearly to take the speck out of your brother's eye."

In this season, focus on being a better you, and stop worrying about everyone else's business. Ask God to create a clean heart in you. Pray for others and leave them in God's hands. They are His masterpiece - not yours!

Judge not lest ye be judged. For with the same judgment ye judge, ye shall be judged: and with what measure ye mete, it shall be measured to you again.

Matthew 7:7

Reflection: Mind your business, pray about the business of others.

Day 41

When people offer criticism - solicited or not - don't be so easily offended. Stop for a moment. It may sting. It may even hurt. But there may be some truth or a lesson to learn in there. Take time to hear.

If they are berating you, cut it. Don't take that in or let it get into your spirit. But if part of what they are saying is actually something that you can take and work on in order to be and do better, heed the wisdom in that.

Even if the delivery wasn't favorable, or it wasn't done in the desired method, you can still learn something from it. Ask the Holy Spirit to give you discernment, and guide you from there.

My son, despise not the chastening of the Lord; neither be weary of His correction: for whom the Lord loveth, he correcteth; even as a father the son in whom he delighteth.

Proverbs 3:11-12

Reflection: Tough conversations are necessary, and are sometimes what you need to wake you up and SHIFT you in the right direction. Process it. Take what you can. Discard what you can't. Shelf the rest for later. You've got this.

Day 42

When we aren't progressing forward or aren't satisfied with our current state of life; it is important to stop and assess where we are spending our time.

Do you sit and watch television or surf social media for hours at a time?

Do you sit and let time just pass you by?

Resting and sitting still to hear God's voice is one thing, but wasting precious time on a regular basis that you could be using to become better, learn a new skill, try a new thing - is another.

The plans of the diligent lead surely to abundance, but everyone who is hasty comes to poverty.
Proverbs 21:5

Reflection: Spend your time wisely. Prioritize what is most important and spend your time accordingly.

Day 43

The decisions that you make today in the present will affect your future self and things that you want to do. Choose and decide wisely so that when you are ready to make moves and step out on faith, today's choices won't negatively impact those results. Be mindful of what you say, what you post, how you say it and who you say it to. The things you put out there digitally are not always erased just because you deleted it.

Let no man despise thy youth, but be thou an example of the believers; in word, in conversation, in charity, in spirit, in faith, in purity.
1 Timothy 4:12

When I was a child, I spake as a child, I understood as a child, I thought as a child: but when I became a man, I put away childish things.
1 Corinthians 13:11

Reflection: Who are you? Be someone your future self will be proud of.

Day 44

Perception and discernment warn us when something is off, out of place, someone needs help, prayer or our time. How often do you heed those warnings? How often do you brush them off? How often is the Holy Spirit trying to tell you something?

The more in tune you are with God, the more you can determine when it is His voice, His guidance, His direction. Sometimes, He is protecting you, and other times, growing you.

"My sheep hear my voice, and I know them, and they follow me."
John 10:27

Reflection: Sit still and reflect on what you are feeling, hearing and "seeing." Don't decide in haste. It could be for right now or for later. Pay close attention.

Day 45

Everything will work out. God's got you. It is my prayer that you have a great day today, that you set the atmosphere around you.

Remember **that those who didn't make you, can't break you. Those who didn't create you, can't negate you**.

You are smart, strong, beautiful, and independent. A phenomenal woman. Walk in your power and strength. And where you are weak, let God be strong in those places for you.

Most gladly therefore will I rather glory in my infirmities, that the power of Christ may rest upon me. Therefore, I take pleasure in infirmities, in reproaches, in necessities, in persecutions, in distresses for Christ's sake: for when I am weak, then am I strong.
2 Corinthians 12:9-10

Reflection: How can you walk in God's power today?

Day 46

A merry heart does good like medicine. When you look around, it is easy to find reasons to be sad, fearful, ungrateful or disappointed. I caution you to change your perspective.

You woke up this morning.
You have breath in your lungs.
A beat in your heart.

The Bible says if we don't praise God, even the rocks will cry out. The sun came up this morning - even if it is hidden behind the clouds. You have a reason to have joy - Jesus is still in control. That in itself is enough to make you shout or just simply smile. Find a reason to laugh. It will elevate your spirit and your mood.

A merry heart doeth good like a medicine: but a broken spirit drieth the bones.
Proverbs 17:22 KJV

Reflection: How will you praise God today?

Day 47

Don't quit. Stay consistent. What you do makes a difference. If God told you to do it, no matter if you are rejected, no matter if no one supports it, no matter if it takes a while to get a client, a sale, a customer, a positive reaction, or forward movement - keep going.

God is faithful and He will see it through to completion. Keep being obedient. **The hike to the top of the mountain is achieved one step at a time**. Don't give up. Keep planting seeds. Let Him handle the harvest. You can do this!

I planted the seed, Apollos watered it, but God made it grow. So neither he who plants nor he who waters is anything, but only God, who makes things grow. The man who plants and the man who waters have one purpose, and each will be rewarded according to his own labor.
1 Corinthians 3:6-8

Reflection: What seeds will you plant or water today?

Day 48

Let all you do be done in love. Not for credit, clout, accolades - but solely as done unto the Lord. Then, what you do in secret, God will reward you openly. The glory is for Him anyway, so don't try to take it or attain it for yourself. Walk in the anointing He has placed on you, and let Him work through you to reach others.

Let all that you do be done with love.
1 Corinthians 16:14

Reflection: When your focus is on Him, you can keep going despite the obstacles in front of you or the opposition you face.

Day 49

Friends are the iron that sharpen us, the anchors that keep us rooted in Christ and uplift us when we are low. If the people in your life aren't adding positive value, cut them loose. In this day and age, life is short, time flies fast and each day has to count. Do away with negativity. You need your mind focused on purpose and being the best version of you. There will always be naysayers, but that doesn't mean that you have to sit and commune with them. No one's voice should be louder than God's. Do they push you towards Him or away from Him? Choose wisely.

Blessed is the man that walketh not in the counsel of the ungodly, nor standeth in the way of sinners, nor sitteth in the seat of the scornful.
Psalm 1:1

Reflection: Elevate your perspective. Get your team right!

Day 50

When you aren't feeling yourself or aren't operating at your best, take time to pause and be mindful of what you are taking in. What is the first thing you reach for? What do you listen to? Be mindful of what you allow into your spirit. What goes in will come out.

If you are listening to a lot of gossip or indulging in a lot of negative news, websites, social media, music - ultimately, you are going to feel and act negatively. Find what inspires, encourages, and uplifts you, so that you can flow in that. Worship music, instructional podcasts, the Bible - what brings YOU joy and passion? There is a time to enjoy certain things, but make sure that you keep your mindset and perspective right.

And Jesus answered him, saying, It is written, that man shall not live by bread alone, but by every word of God.
Luke 4:4

Reflection: Feed your soul daily. Your life depends on it.

Day 51

Self Care Is The Best Care! No matter what you do, taking care of yourself is extremely important. Getting enough sleep, drinking enough water, getting some exercise - all contribute to helping you to be the best version of yourself. If you aren't taking care of you - you can't properly care for anyone else. Your mental, physical, spiritual, emotional and financial health all matter. God wants us to prosper and be in good health even as our soul prospers.

Beloved, I wish above all things that thou mayest prosper and be in health, even as thy soul prospereth.
3 John 1:2

Reflection: What are you doing TODAY to take better care of yourself?!

Day 52

Running isn't the answer. That is usually the easy way out. Planning and executing a plan to make change is a better way. Does it make you uncomfortable? Yes. Do you have to be patient and wait? Yes. But there is purpose and power in the waiting. Oftentimes, it is building your character, strength, stamina and persistence. Don't quit and run when things are tough. Stand your ground, hold on to those roots, and weather the storm. God's got you.

And Moses said unto the people, fear ye not, stand still, and see the salvation of the Lord, which He will shew to you today: for the Egyptians whom ye have seen today, ye shall see them again no more forever.
Exodus 14:13

Reflection: Put on your whole armor and fight. The enemy you see today, you will see no more!

Day 53

Knowing your why keeps you motivated and moving towards your goals. When you can't define your why, it makes doing your work and serving others that much harder. You have a purpose and value that you bring to others.

What drives you to keep going, to do better and be better? Defining that will help fuel your passion and persistence, even when things are tough. Don't let the temporary feelings of yesterday prevent you from being the best version of you today. If you aren't sure of your why, start with the Who.

The Lord will perfect that which concerneth me: thy mercy, O Lord, endureth for ever: forsake not the works of Thine own hands.
Psalm 138:8

Reflection: Who do you do it for? Yourself, your family, God? Start there and keep moving forward.

Day 54

Whether you have a lot or a little, abound or are in lack, when you trust God, He will take care of you and your every need - now or later. When you give to others - your time, your love, sacrifice, money, your presence - you are sowing seeds into them that you will reap a harvest from. So keep trusting God and keep planting seeds.

Seek ye first the kingdom of God and His righteousness and everything else will be added unto you.
Matthew 6:33
Give and it shall be given you, good measure, pressed down, shaken together and running over shall men give unto your bosom.
Luke 6:38

Reflection: God will take care of you. Though He tarries, wait for Him. He will show up and show out!

Day 55

What has God been pushing you to do? Telling you to do? What desire is burning inside and won't go away? What is stopping you from taking the leap of faith and going after it?! If God gave you the green light to go, the time is now. You may have been waiting on God, but guess what? He's waiting on you! Jump! Leap! Step out on faith. Keep God first and let everything that you do be done in love. God's got you!

A man's gifts maketh room for him, and bringeth him before great men.
Proverbs 18:16

Reflection: Take steps today to walk out what He's given you to do! Let your gift make room for you.

Day 56

There are some things that you do - give, serve, love. At times, it may feel that your sacrifice goes unnoticed and seems like a thankless role. Be encouraged. God sees everything that you do - every seed that you plant when you give of yourself, your time, your gifts. You will still reap a harvest on those seeds. So continue to plant them in love, even if you never get the thank you that you desired.
How often does God do stuff on our behalf, and we say thank you?

But to do good and to communicate, forget not: for with such sacrifices God is well pleased.
Hebrews 13:16

Reflection: Serve in love and leave the rest to God.

Day 57

You are a work in progress. You always will be along this journey called life. Take off the pressure of perfection. Trust God to teach you, mold and guide you. Approach each day as your best self and continue to push to be better. As you learn and grow, share what you have learned with others, so that they can do and be better, too.

No one has it all figured out or has it all together. That's why you must continually return to your Creator and allow Him to reset and adjust you. The key is to stay connected to Him. Surrender your life to Him. And let your every footstep, words, actions, speech and deeds be done unto Him. Then, your way will be prosperous and His light will shine through you.

For God who commanded the light to shine out of darkness, hath shined in our hearts, to give the light of the knowledge of the glory of God in the face of Jesus Christ. But we have this treasure in earthen vessels, that the excellency of the power may be of God, and not of us.
2 Corinthians 4:6-7

Reflection: Raise the level of your perspective.

Day 58

Even when you are facing storms or trouble all around you, keep your focus on God. He is bigger and greater than any storm in your life. Some of God's greatest miracles happened in the midst of storms - because the people prepared BEFORE the storm. Noah and Ark. Joshua in Jericho. Moses and the Red Sea. Even Jesus and the Cross. What is God preparing you for? Even if no one else believes or understands, don't let that stop the instructions that you were given.

He that dwells in the secret place of the most High, shall abide under the shadow of the Almighty. I will say of the Lord, He alone is my refuge, my fortress; my God, in Him will I trust.
Psalm 91:1-2

Reflection: Abide in God. Trust Him at His word.

Day 59

NOTHING is impossible for you. Read that again. Dare to dream. Dare to believe. What have you wanted to do, desired to do, or maybe even previously tried to do that has not happened yet? What is too hard for you to do on your own but you know that you were made to do it? Today, I want you to imagine yourself fulfilling that goal. There is no limit to what you can do, if you just believe.

But Jesus beheld them, and said unto them, with men this is impossible; but with God, all things are possible.
Matthew 19:26

Reflection: Trust God to meet you there. You can and you will!

Day 60

As you go about your day today, think about the goodness of God. Some days are regularly full and busy, but His grace is sufficient to sustain and keep you. This is a great day that He has made and He has equipped you for such a time as this. Pick your three highest priority tasks and focus on completing those things first. After that, if time allows, work on the other lower priority tasks. You will be less anxious and accomplish more.

Be careful for nothing; but in everything, by prayer and supplication, with thanksgiving, let your requests be made known unto God. And the peace of God, which passeth all understanding, shall keep your hearts and minds through Christ Jesus.
Philippians 4:6-7

Reflection: Focus on your top three priorities.

Day 61

When you woke up this morning, how did you view today?! Were you ready and motivated? Energized and ready to go? How you view your day and yourself matters. As you think in your heart, so are you. You will get what you expect and what you think. Make sure that you are expecting positive things to happen and that you see yourself in a positive light - despite what is happening around you.

For as he thinketh in his heart, so is he: eat and drink, saith he to thee; but his heart is not with thee.
Proverbs 23:7

Reflection: It all starts with your mindset. You matter.

Day 62

Feelings are real and it is okay - best - to acknowledge them and that they are there. Don't discount or ignore your feelings. Sometimes, they are a discernment of danger or a warning in your spirit. Sometimes, they are there to distract you and break your focus.

No matter what feelings you are having, don't lose sight of the One who can do something with those feelings and emotions. God is always worthy of your praise and adoration. As you process through your feelings, thank Him for being right there with you. Tell Him how you feel and find encouragement in the fact that His love for you will only grow stronger, even if your current feelings aren't so fond of Him. Is that not incredible?! Nothing will decrease His love for you.

But thou, O Lord, art a shield for me; my glory, and the lifter up of mine head.
Psalm 3:3

Reflection: Tell Him how you honestly feel and let Him lift your head.

Day 63

Have you ever woken up with anxiety, but you can't quite pinpoint why? Or you have an inkling, but aren't fully sure if that's it? Rather than become frantic or panic, take a deep breath. Having anxiety is okay; it's how you react or respond next that matters. Talk to God about it. Talk to a counselor or a trusted friend that can help pray you through it. Where two or three are gathered in His name, He is there in the midst. One can put one thousand to flight, but two can put ten thousand to flight. In other words, there is strength in numbers.

For where two or three are gathered together in my name, there am I in the midst of them.
Matthew 18:20

Reflection: You don't have to do this journey alone. Allow God to settle your heart.

Day 64

Sometimes we make a big deal out of things that really aren't that big of a deal. When you stop to think about it, and look at the bigger picture, you realize that you are giving too much time and energy to things that you either can't change or aren't as important as you thought it was. Take time to step back and breathe. Be grateful. Notice the positive things. Try listing three good things happening in your life. When you focus on the bigger picture and the more positive aspects, you attract more of those positive things and worry less about the little stuff.

But they that wait upon the Lord shall renew their strength; they shall mount up with wings as eagles; they shall run, and not be weary; and they shall walk, and not faint.
Isaiah 40:31

Reflection: focus on the bigger picture.

Day 65

God isn't through with you yet! You are a work in progress and will spend a lifetime becoming who He created you to be. Your mistakes, and the opinions of others, do not define you. Only God's word and His truth define you. So get to know Him and His word - if you really want to know the truth about who you are. Learn and share what you've learned. If they didn't make you, they can't break you. If they didn't create you, they can't negate you.

Before I formed thee in the belly I knew thee; and before thou camest forth out of the womb, I sanctified thee, and I ordained thee a prophet unto the nations.
Jeremiah 1:5

Reflection: Know Whose you are. Never forget.

Day 66

How are you feeling today? No. I mean really. Behind the mask. Behind the smile. On the inside where no one but God can see. How's your heart and mindset? If it doesn't match what you are showing on the outside, it's okay. All days aren't rainbows and sunshine. It does get better.

You know what else? Jesus still loves you. He is walking with you every step of the way. So be encouraged. Enjoy the physical sun shining on your face. Listen to the birds or sounds of nature.

Casting all your anxieties on him, because he cares for you.
1 Peter 5:7

Reflection: Find your place of peace and don't let anyone take it away.

Day 67

Guess what? Today is going to be a great day! You've already made up in your mind that you are going to make the most of today and the gift of life that God has given you. You are going to be a blessing to other people. You are going to make wise decisions and better choices.

You will know in your spirit which way to go and you will be confident in and stand by that decision. You will speak peace and joy to everyone you interact with and you will set the temperature around you. Being cautious who you allow in; staying away from those who want their negativity to latch on to you. Nope! Not today!

You are walking in power and anointing and you know who you are - even if you are still learning day by day. Don't allow anyone else to define it but you and God.

For we are His workmanship, created in Christ Jesus unto good works, which God hath ordained that we should walk in them.
Ephesians 2:10

Reflection: Own who you are - a work in progress, yet valuable, wise and powerful! Know Whose You Are!!!!!

Day 68

Always make sure you have a voice. You matter. Your input and opinion matter. Don't let anyone else silence you or keep you from speaking up. Stand up for yourself and for others. Be tactful. Be respectful. Speak from a place of grace and compassion. Speak truth. Let people know where they stand with you. Treat them how you want to be treated. You only get one shot at this thing called life.

She openeth her mouth with wisdom; and in her tongue is the law of kindness.
Proverbs 31:26

Reflection: Be bold and be true. Just Be You.

Day 69

Some things, you just can't control. Life happens and you have to roll with it. Take a deep breath. Relax. Pivot. Keep going. It will work out the way it is supposed to, even if that looks different than you originally planned. The power and strength in being adaptable is of great value - anyone can quit when things don't go as planned - but when you can improvise, adapt and overcome - that is when you will see and achieve the best results.
Don't be so stuck to your plan that you miss the hints along the way that show you which direction to go. Enjoy the journey and path to the destination, no matter what it looks like. Oh, and if the destination ends up changing as you go along, that is okay.

And your ears shall hear a word behind you, saying, "This is the way, walk in it," when you turn to the right or when you turn to the left.
Isaiah 30:21

Reflection: Accept it and grow.

Day 70

As humans, we have constant interactions with others. People come into our lives - for various lengths of time, some long, some short. As we begin to grow, change or stretch, some people are removed from our lives. Sometimes, a friendship may end, a relationship, or a business partnership.

Wisdom will teach you that everyone can't go with you. As you step into your destiny, you will have to let go of some people so that you can thrive and be your best self. And you can't always do that while still holding on to the same people, the same patterns, the same habits, and the same mindset. The cutting away hurts for a while, but it is truly to make you better so that you can rise higher and have the wisdom to handle it when it comes. As you step into this day, hold on to God, who never changes.

Jesus Christ, the same yesterday, and today, and forever.
Hebrews 13:8

Reflection: Let God be the constant in your life and trust Him every step of the way - including with every connection He makes or breaks.

Day 71

The verse of the day today stuck with me. Especially in the amplified version because of one word - consistently. As humans, we are inevitably imperfect. But every day we have an opportunity to try again. Each day is a present - or gift - to us to do and be better. The more you consistently strive for that and reach for God, the better you become. He must be your first priority above ALL others. Whether it is five minutes or just one prayer - do it as consistently as you can, and grow from there.

Blessed and favored by God are those who keep His testimonies, and who consistently seek Him and long for Him with all their heart.
Psalm 119:2 AMP

Reflection: God's got you. Make sure you have Him, too.

Day 72

Let me paint a picture for you this morning! You woke up this morning. You have a beat in your heart and breath in your lungs. You have another opportunity at life. If you have shelter, food, clothes on your back, transportation - yours or ride share - a job or a legal means to make an income - then, you are blessed and highly favored of the Lord! You have a reason to praise God. A reason to lift your head. A reason to be encouraged, grateful, thankful. What will you do today to express that gratitude and to make an impact on someone else?!

Give thanks to the LORD, for he is good. His love endures forever.
Psalm 136:1

Reflection: What will you do with the gift of today? Make it count.

Day 73

Prayer changes things! That thing you went to sleep thinking about last night. That thing that was on your mind when you woke up this morning. That you carry all throughout the day. Pray about those things. And then, leave it alone. Trust God to work it out. Don't pick it back up if He doesn't do it in your timing either. Either you trust Him to handle it or you don't. Resist the urge to take His place trying to do it yourself. He will work it out according to His plan - even if it looks differently than you wanted.

Elijah was a man subject to like passions as we are, and he prayed earnestly that it might not rain: and it rained not on the earth by the space of three years and six months. And he prayed again, and the heaven gave rain, and the earth brought forth her fruit.
James 5:17-18

Reflection: Let go and maintain your peace. Pray about it and leave it in God's hands!

Day 74

It is a beautiful morning! The sun and the full moon are both out! Hopefully, you can see clearly today. Whether you have much or whether you have little, learn to be content in whatever state you are in. Be a blessing to someone else and celebrate right where you are right now. Phone a friend. Share a hug or a smile. Let someone know that you care. We are all in this together and we can't do life alone. On this day, it is my prayer that you know that you are not alone and no matter what your current reality looks like, there is always hope.

Not that I speak in respect of want: for I have learned, in whatsoever state I am, therewith to be content. I know both how to be abased, and I know how to abound: everywhere and in all things I am instructed both to be full and to be hungry, both to abound and to suffer need. I can do all things through Christ which strengtheneth me.
Philippians 4:11-13

Reflection: You matter. You are loved. You are enough. Just Be You.

Day 75

Trust is one of the most important components and foundation of any relationship. Without it, it is very difficult - almost impossible - to move the relationship forward. Many times we view our relationship with God in direct relation to the relationships that we have experienced here on earth and our expectations of God - or lack thereof - mimic what we are familiar with.

The problem with that is that we can't base God's nature and character on the choices of other humans. God is not human. He is the Supreme being that we are to pattern ourselves after. He is the same yesterday, today and forever. Because of that, we can put our trust in Him and have total faith that He will do everything that He said He would.

For I am persuaded, that neither death, nor life, nor angels, nor principalities, nor powers, nor things present, nor things to come, nor height, nor depth, nor any other creature, shall be able to separate us from the love of God, which is in Christ Jesus our Lord.
Romans 8:38-39

Reflection: Get to know God by spending time talking to Him and reading His word. Build that trust in Him. He's got you. He will always love you - unconditionally.

Day 76

I just wanted to pop in real quick and tell you something important! Guess what? You are AMAZING! You Matter! You are Loved! You are Enough! You must tell yourself that every single day! Don't allow anyone to tell you anything different. These things remain at all times. You are so loved that a Man laid down his life for you! No matter what happens in life. No matter what anyone else says. Never forget Whose you are! The ultimate sacrifice was paid for you. Walk out each day knowing that you are valuable, important and loved unconditionally! No matter what mistakes you have made, are currently making or will make - it doesn't change the truth of who you are.

Greater love hath no man than this, that a man lay down his life for his friends.
John 15:13

Reflection: Let that be your hope and focus as you go through your day!

Day 77

Heart check. Today, check your heart. Out of the abundance of the heart, the mouth speaks. Be mindful of what you are allowing and putting in, so that what flows out is truly representative of you - genuine and authentic. Strive to Just Be You - the best version that you can be every day. Speak life to yourself and those around you. There is the power of life and death in your tongue.

Death and life are in the power of the tongue: and they that love it shall eat the fruit thereof.
Proverbs 18:21

O generation of vipers, how can ye, being evil, speak good things? For out of the abundance of the heart, the mouth speaketh. A good man out of the good treasure of the heart bringeth forth good things: and an evil man out of the evil treasure bringeth forth evil things. But I say unto you, that every idle word that men shall speak, they shall give account thereof in the day of judgment. For by thy words thou shalt be justified, and by thy words, thou shalt be condemned.
Matthew 12:34-37

Reflection: Watch your words.

Day 78

What are you grateful for today? For the people in your life, make sure that you tell them. For life, thank God. For everything else, be grateful. Share a meal, a smile, shelter, warmth. Life is a journey and it takes us all working together along the way. I am grateful for you, and pray that you have a blessed day today.

O give thanks unto the Lord; for He is good: for His mercy endureth forever.
Psalm 136:1

Reflection: Be grateful and give thanks for everything in your life.

Day 79

At this exact time one week ago, I was involved in a major car accident. Saying I am thankful to be alive is an understatement. All week I have hugged a little tighter and longer. I have enjoyed being in the moment. I have taken time to rest and to appreciate the simple things. Life passes by so fast and can end just as quickly. When I say make each day count, treasure the ones you love and tell people what they mean to you - listen. It's for a reason. Don't take for granted that you will see them again or that they will just be there when you get home. Don't be too busy to care or to speak or to notice them.

Therefore do not be anxious about tomorrow, for tomorrow will be anxious for itself. Sufficient for the day is its own trouble.
Matthew 6:34

Reflection: You matter and the people around you do, too.

Day 80

Rise and shine! Give God glory! Time to jump into the day and keep bringing value to everyone around you. No matter what you do or what you are facing today, remember that someone needs what you have. Their next step depends on how you show up. So show up as your best self and give it your best shot. Smile. Shake a hand. Give a hug. A ride. Show yourself friendly. You may be the only positive that someone sees today, and it may bring them hope.

Worthy are you, our Lord and God, to receive glory and honor and power, for you created all things, and by your will they existed and were created.
Psalm 115:1

Reflection: Have a fabulous day today and maintain your joy and peace!

Day 81

When you were a child, playing was second nature. As you get older, work and responsibilities take precedence. Today, I want to remind you to take time to play. You only get one shot at life. Don't let it pass you by and at the end say you worked a lot. Instead, be able to say you made the most of your time and though you worked hard, you also played hard. Use your imagination and get back to the basics.

He that followeth after righteousness and mercy findeth life,
righteousness, and honor.
Proverbs 21:21

Reflection: A better you is waiting.

Day 82

Life is literally passing by; it appears to be going faster nowadays. Spend time with the ones you love most. Apologize. Make it right. While you still can. Don't hold grudges or harbor anger or resentment. There's no time to waste on that. There's no time waste period. Let people know that you love them. Treat them right. Don't sweat the small stuff. Walk together. Hold one another up. Share the love of Jesus. You may be the only reflection of Him that people see. Make your dash count and count your blessings.

Wherefore putting away lying, speak every man truth with his neighbor: for we are members one of another. Be ye angry, and sin not: let not the sun go down upon your wrath: neither give place to the devil.
Ephesians 4:25-27

Reflection: If you're still here, you still have purpose. Fulfill it.

Day 83

A merry heart does good like a medicine. That means that no matter what you are walking through or facing each day, if you keep your heart in check, you can still have peace and joy. Life will happen and not always according to our plan, but if we keep the right motives and focus on the things above, we can wake up every day ready to try again; we can have hope for a brighter day and we can stand firm in our faith. When you can find laughter and joy, it automatically makes you feel better - even if but for a moment - kind of like medicine. What makes you laugh? What puts a smile on your face? Partake in more of that and raise the level of your joy.

A merry heart doeth good like a medicine: but a broken spirit drieth the bones.
Proverbs 17:22

Reflection: There is still good in this world. Limit the negative, focus on the positive.

Day 84

When you are feeling heavy, remember that God is there. He's got you. You are not alone. The things that you can't control. The times that you don't know how or even why. You always know Who. And He is the same yesterday, today and forevermore. Find hope and comfort in that.

Cast all your cares on Him, because He cares for you.
1 Peter 5:7

Reflection: God is the steady in the midst of change.

Day 85

What's next? Do you have a plan? For your day, your week, your year, your life? Without a vision, the people perish. Each day, you should have one to three main things that you need to do to keep moving you forward. Every step counts. If you don't have a plan, how will you know where you are going? Make a plan and stick to it. Even if you get off course for a bit, find your way back, adjust and keep working the plan! The possibilities are endless.

Where there is no vision, the people perish: but he that keepeth the law, happy is he.
Proverbs 29:18

Reflection: what is your vision for this next stage of your life?

Day 86

Did you know that God's approval is the only One that you need? If no one else says thank you for the things that you have done. If no one else approves of your dream or desires or believes in it like you. If you are your biggest fan and loudest cheerleader. **The ONLY approval or applause that matters - is God's.** He trumps all others. So don't let a lack of gratitude from those you serve stop you from serving. Do it with a smile and joy in your heart. God will reward you. He will bless the work of your hands.

What shall we say to these things? If God be for us, who can be against us? He that spared not His own Son, but delivered Him up for us all, how shall He not with him also freely give us all things?
Romans 8:31-32

Reflection: So let ALL you do be done in love and done as unto the Lord.

Day 87

You aren't at your best when you're tired. It's important - critical - that you get the proper rest that you need. So that you can wake up refreshed and present the best version of yourself. Don't go too many days without truly resting. While you are sleeping, your body repairs itself and restores and renews and refreshes. Go to bed at a decent time; put down your phones and turn off the television. Allow your mind to rest so that your body can physically rest. Self care is the best care.

The Lord is my shepherd; I shall not want. He maketh me to lie down in green pastures: He leadeth me beside the still waters. He restoreth my soul: He leadeth me in the path of righteousness for His name's sake.
Psalm 23:1-3

Reflection: There are only 24 hours in a day. Plan wisely.

Day 88

Are the people that you are surrounding yourself with making you better or not? Are you able to be your true authentic self, or do you find yourself putting on heirs or trying to be someone other than yourself? Are you picking up bad habits or feeling drained every time that you leave from their presence? Surround yourself with people who push you to be the best version of you; who accept you as you are, but have a genuine care to see you become a better person. Not for their own personal gain, but because they want what is best for you. You must make the most of each day. Be mindful of who you are giving or devoting your time to. If they are negatively affecting you, let them go. You matter. You are loved. You are enough. Just be you.

For if, after they have escaped the defilements of the world through the knowledge of our Lord and Savior Jesus Christ, they are again entangled in them and overcome, the last state has become worse for them than the first.
2 Peter 2:20

Now the Lord is the Spirit, and where the Spirit of the Lord is, there is freedom.
2 Corinthians 3:17

Reflection: You are a reflection of who you spend the most time with. Is it a reflection that you are proud of?

Day 89

Today, I am reminded of when Jesus visits Martha and Mary. Martha is busy hosting and cooking, while Mary sits at the feet of Jesus. Martha becomes annoyed and frustrated with Mary for not helping her, but Jesus says that Mary has chosen the right thing. So today, I caution you to not get caught up in the day to day tasks that are always there; that you forget to do the best thing, which is to spend time with God and to take care of yourself so that you can then pour out to others. You can't pour from an empty vessel, and if you are serving,working,cooking,cleaning - begrudgingly, why bother anyway? There is no reward in that. Love God. Love yourself. Love others. Always in that order. Be about your Father's business. He will give you the strength to complete the rest.

And He said unto them, how is it that ye sought Me? Wist ye not that I must be about my Father's business?
Luke 2:49

And Jesus answered and said unto her, Martha, Martha, thou art careful and troubled about many things: but one thing is needful: and Mary hath chosen that good part, which shall not be taken away from her.
Luke 10:41-42

Reflection: Let God help you prioritize the tasks of the day.

Day 90

Oftentimes, we don't have the answers; nor do we understand why things happen a certain way. Some things are above our level of natural reasoning and can only be seen or understood in the spiritual realm. Whatever you are carrying, whatever answers you didn't get, closure you didn't attain, or understanding that never came - lean into God. He is the same yesterday, today, and forever. He doesn't change. Even when you don't know why, when, how, what or where - you always know Who.

I will instruct thee and teach thee in the way which thou shalt go: I will guide thee with mine eye.
Psalm 32:8

Reflection: Hold to God's unchanging hand. He will see you through.

About the Author

Tonia D Benas is a lover of life! Her greatest passion is empowering others to become all that God has created them to be. She is a wife and mother of 5 children, and has one grandson as well. She strives to make her dash count and positively impact others on a daily basis. She enjoys the beach, being outdoors, camping, and all things DIY. Woodworking is one of her favorite DIY projects to do, and she has created quite a few awesome pieces of furniture and built ins, a deck, and a vast array of signs and home decor. She is a Realtor, a certified notary, and an advocate for diversity and inclusion. She enjoys sharing lessons that she has learned or is in the midst of learning, so that hopefully, it can help someone else to be and do better as well.

She is also the founder of The Journey of You, an online community that is dedicated to empowering women to become all that God has created them to be, and to truly be the best version of themselves. You can join the community: https://www.whereyourlifebegins.com

Include social media and website information.
IG: @toniadbenas
IG: @signsdesignsanddecor
Tumblr: https://toniadbenas.tumblr.com
www.toniadbenas.com

Other books by Tonia D Benas:

Love Letters
I am Special, What God Thinks of Me
RVU: Butterfly

Coming Soon:
Infectious Teenager
Infectious Parents
Infectious Leaders
Infectious Choices
Two Thirds of Me

Sources

1 Randi Chanel Person; conversation on January 3, 2013 10:12am